AF668274

Land of a Thousand Muses

by

Christopher Hivner

Copyright© 2025 Christopher Hivner
ISBN: 978-93-6354-498-7

First Edition: 2025
Rs. 200/-

Cyberwit.net
HIG 45 Kaushambi Kunj, Kalindipuram
Allahabad - 211011 (U.P.) India
http://www.cyberwit.net
Tel: +(91) 9415091004
E-mail: info@cyberwit.net

No part of this book may be reproduced or transmitted in any form or by any means, electronic, mechanical, photocopying, or otherwise, without the express written consent of Christopher Hivner.

Printed at Vcore.

Dedication

For my brother Woody who supported me

every day and left this world too soon

In any artistic field, a muse is a source of inspiration for the artist, influencing their work by generating new ideas. A muse could be a person, an object, or almost anything that sparks the artist's dormant imagination. The word is derived from Greek and Roman mythology where the Muses were goddesses who inspired man in the arts and sciences.

This collection spotlights ten different muses I used to write my poems.

Contents

Muse 1

Art

(all of the paintings or photos I was inspired by can be found on the internet if you want to study them)

Drinking in the Dusk

inspired by Street in Venice *by John Singer Sargent*

Windows blink black,
the air breathes perfume,
the sun lays low
in the mortar
of the stone
yet still
there are shadows
hiding hooded eyes
in lined faces,
winks passed
as coded language,
collars are turned up
against the cold
as well as to cover
leers that could cut.

She departs from her lover
to find a way home,
doors are closed,
eyes lowered,
the swish, swish
of her dress
find the men
between drags of
hand-rolled cigarettes.
They look and dream,
smile before closing their eyes,

she pulls the shawl tighter
over thin shoulders,
their desire
a cold finger
to her spine.

Windows drop black,
houses drink in dusk,
the old women on the corner
remember their own days
of wine and embraces.
They know where
she's come from
because they visited
the same door,
knocked with the same hand,
displayed the same flesh.
In their youth
they were her,
owned by the temptations
of the street.

The Boatman

inspired by Houses of Parliament, Sunset *by Claude Monet*

The boatman skimmed the water
broken shafts of sunlight
buoying his craft
as he traced the shadows.

The buildings loomed
stealing the dying light
to hold for tomorrow,
their reflections
river monsters in repose.

The lapping of the water
against the hull
carried the captain
to home,
calm reassurance
he was where he
was supposed to be.

With a wink
to the ministers on shore
he prayed
they did their job
as well as
he did his.

Sun setting,
another day ending,
the boatman skimmed the water
reaching for the horizon
on the other side
of the shadows.

Presence

inspired by La Scapigliata (Female Head), *by Leonardo da Vinci*

Above and below the stars
there is my testimony to you,
divine worship strung like pearls
from destiny to fantasy through
the ocean of the milky way.

My dream, my temptation, my seduction,
turn your face toward my longing,
open your eyes to me on my knees,
weave your hair around me
a bed for me to yearn from,
tangle my arms and legs,
strings to make me dance at your touch.

Seasons pass in your eyes,
words of healing live on your lips,
if I could stroke your cheek
with the back of my hand
I would become tangible,
my soul languid and revolutionary.

I want to exist in your presence,
I need to exist.

Wine of the Day

inspired by Ship of Fools *by Hieronymus Bosch*

We flew the banner
of the fading moon
as we set sail
through the forest
of fools.
We gave full throat
to our song,
our sailing elegy,
our morning gray-sky entreaty
to the festival gods.
Drink from the cup,
only a sip,
drink the wine of the day,
vinegar and sugar,
sugar and spirits,
enough to fuel
our broken ship
for the promised land.
Wake up helmsman!
Wake up!
Steer us righteous,
the others are waiting
for our arrival.
We've brought
Bacchus and Terpsichore
along for the ride
to support our trip

to the river run.
We fly the banner
of ignorance and hubris,
our boat a sinking forest
for the trees.
Drink from the cup
our wine of the day,
vinegar and tree sap,
selfishness and lost dreams.

12:43

Inspired by Time Transfixed *by Rene Magritte*

12:43
The stillness
covers my skin like grime,
I absent-mindedly scratch
the palm of my hand
entreating money to come my way
according to the
old wives' tale.
After,
the quiet regains control.

12:43
The train whistle echoes
off the walls
disturbing the peace
but it's for a good reason
as the 550 from New York
is pulling in,
bringing with it
life.

12:43
I'm supposed to be on
the 550,
coming home
to sparse reality.
but I missed the connection.

and I've yet to arrive.
The conductor
is not concerned.

12:43
The clock ticks,
a torturous tune
boring into my ears
as I await the movement
of the long hand,
the extension of time,
the foretelling of the future,
the continuation
of all things cosmic.

12:43
The stillness in the room
is a susurration
of no consensus.
The reflections in the mirror
are a cheshire cat grin
in response to knowing
the unseen door
will not open,
the ante room
is an anti-room
and the constancy
begins with

12:43

The Spectral Foam

inspired by Full Fathom Five *by Jackson Pollak*

Spellbound river of abstract green
flowing through a map
of generations,
I can't immortalize
the creature I've become
without strings of fantasy.

Follow me north,
through the gate
that leads,
the gate that will bring
you to me
on a misplaced line,
the doorway to where
I used to be.

I can feel
the teeth sinking in,
your bite draws blood
from my dead veins,
your countenance looms
over my city
as spiraling black and gold,
follow my spectral foam
down river.

We won't find each other
in this maze,
likely for the best,
I'm not the man
I used to be,
and you never deserved the glory anyway.

Follow the river,
forget my words,
I am under
and can't surface.

Outpost

Inspired by Railroad Sunset *by Edward Hopper*

There was nothing to look at
except grass and a
setting sun sky
that flared like
a campfire.
The train passed
an outpost
and even that was deserted,
the master gone home
to supper with the wife.
Yet here we were
a few dozen salty travelers
on an ancient train,
the 910 to
here, there and everywhere,
arriving back home late,
the angry horizon
swallowing the train
as we roll along the tracks.
I have no one waiting
at the station
which colors my mood,
makes me think less of the
rollicking cars
and the disappearing sun.
The man across the aisle
is snoring with a

devil-may-care attitude
I've never had.
I can finally see the station
in the distance,
sitting up straighter
I take a final look
at the landmark-less rolling hills
to say goodbye
and wait,
the loneliness easing upward
like acid from my stomach.
I got on the train by myself,
will depart the same
and drive home alone
to a dark, prosaic house
that will greet me
with silence.
My earlier annoyance
with the train being off schedule
fades while I pray
for a breakdown
or obstruction on the tracks,
my neighbor's snoring
suddenly an analgesic.
The train begins to slow,
I look at the last sliver
of the sun
above the horizon.
Then it's gone,
the train stops,
the man across from me
wakes up,
time to go.

Overnight

inspired by Night Train *by Gerrie Paino*

Galaxies of stars
sending light my way
from the past,
I won't be here
when it arrives.

A delivery of photons
were dropped off yesterday
for my brother,
but he's been gone
since last year,
so I signed for them
to keep in my pocket
and let the heat
bring him alive again
even if for
just a moment.

Muse 2

poems written by coming up with a title first

A Brief Interruption

I have been made irrelevant

by layoffs and rejections,
form letters and non-replies,
haughty, indifferent felines,
telephone solicitors who don't
know when to quit,
check engine lights that won't go off
and noises from somewhere that
get louder, but won't reveal their location
with a mechanic present,
television announcers who make
in one year what would take me twenty
and still don't know what
they're talking about,
politicians that talk and talk and talk
and talk and talk and talk.

I have been interrupted

in my quest for fulfillment,
in my daily lecture series
to no one in particular
about things that annoy me,
in my search for inspiration,
during a longed for
good night's sleep,
by a friend with a problem
I have no solution to,

in the middle of a prayer,
during a good conversation,
by an answer
I wasn't expecting.

These moments of life

have stalled my progress,
chased dreams from my yard,
refused to do the dishes
that are piling up in the sink,
left me laughing uncontrollably,
gave me stories to tell
to people who didn't care
but listened amiably anyway
from the supermarket check-out line,
have found me face down and in tears,
led me to question everything,
gave me purpose.

Broad Shoulders

I have broad shoulders.
My grandma used to say
I could play football
without the pads
because that's the
kind of thing
grandmothers say.
I have broad shoulders
but sometimes
the weight
settles in my bones
and I sag
into the earth
consumed by
all and everything.
A voice or thought
or a desire
wakes me up
from a dark and bold reverie
to ignite my will.
I climb
brushing the rancid earth
from my body
to ease the pressure.
My grandma probably
would have said
I could carry the world
without help
because that's what
grandmas say.

A Good Spot

This is where
I can talk to you,
under the Carolina blue sky,
in front of the
straight-trunked trees,
limbs full of leaves
waving in the breeze.

This is where
I long for you
to not be gone,
to not be
laid out in the six feet
of ground below.
I need you to hear
the cardinals sing again,
to close your eyes
and feel the sun
cleanse your skin.

This is where
I speak to you now,
lamentations in a whisper,
doe-eyed stares into the sky,
legs unsteady.
There is beauty here,
but it's missing you
with your lopsided smile.

This is a good spot,
close to others
so you're not alone,
I remember how
you hated being alone.
The grass is sparkling green
and the trees stand
as protectors,
fending off the shadows.

It's a good spot
that I wish
I didn't have to visit,
but I do
to feel your presence
in this world
you left behind.

The Letter Was Late Getting to Me

Past and future
control my present
in ways that leave me
walking the neighborhood
listening to genres
of music
I don't understand
to see the whole universe
in the trees
swaying in the wind.

I wrote myself a letter
when I was
in the tenth grade
telling me
to grow some balls
and move on,
let shit go,
fantasize not fetishize,
make a plan,
forget what he did
and didn't do.

Rescue can come
from other people,
but it's just as easy
for the door to click shut
behind you.
Time spent

with someone else
may buy you
the clue you need,
or she might be
a redux
of restless nights
sleeping instead of breathing.

Forty years on
I'm still looking
for absolution
from the mistake I made,
an explanation
of the grievance,
a meeting
that can't happen
with the ashes having
been carried by the fluttering breeze
to the island
no one can reach
from the future
or the present.

Leave Monday Behind

The weekend stole the air
from my lungs,
the gloom of the empty house
settled on my skin,
pinching the blood
from my veins.
The hours crept
down the hallway
pulling the floorboards up
as they went,
the crack of the wood
kept me awake
more than the lack of oxygen
in my lungs.

I waited,
and I lost.
I prayed
and time broke.
The TV couldn't
cut through the pall
of the prison walls.
The silence
pulled me from the air.
I was alive
because my skin crawled
with pincers,
I was dead
because I didn't care.

I stayed.
I waited until you came home,
but it wasn't the you
I wanted,
you were someone else,
biting, acid-lipped,
unrepentant.

Now I have to leave Monday behind
diving into Tuesday
searching for the version
of you
that left for the weekend
without a word,
searching for myself as well,
because I haven't existed
since Friday night.

End to End

Wishing for it
is the first step
in the manual,
page three
after the introduction,
written by the person
you want to be.
Dreaming,
which is different than wishing,
is the catalyst,
the fuse
trailing for days or miles
depending on your point of view.
Manifesting is the grind,
day after night after day,
through the 2 p.m. staff meeting
Larry is always late for,
past the bank account
with the mean numbers
that taunt you
with toothless mouths
and laughter
like a mower
that won't start.
Believe.
Wish, dream, believe,
every day and night,
on the toilet,
during calls from mom,

lay it all end to end
and one day,
peace.

Muse 3

A prompt given to you by a third party

prompt: written in a surreal style, what do you dream when you dream of animals

Come to the Cathedral

Dreams
make my blood deep red
*Dream*s
rebuild my senses
Dreams
bring the tigers

In dreams
I don't run from the tigers
In dreams
the animals talk, but I don't
In dreams
everywhere is home

Without dreams
my walk is slow
Without dreams
I do run from tigers
Without dreams
my blood cools

Dreams
color the world electric blue
Dreams
bring the tigers home to me
Dreams
turn the light on in the dark

prompt: poems written "of surf and sand"

Shifting

I would run forever
along the wet sand
if I knew
the water wouldn't
try to consume me,
if the beach
wouldn't fall away,
collapsing around my feet.
Each step I take
is a reminder
of the edge
I walk,
the line that separates
my world
from yours
and hers and his.
I could run forever
if I knew the line
wouldn't move
and pull me along with it.

prompt: Make a wish (written in a fantasy style)

Alchemy

I wanted her
to not be there,
"for once," I asked aloud
"don't disappoint me."
But the door opened
and she stepped out
in another man's arms.

In the darkness of the alley
I stared
at the fairy dust
in my hand,
the same magic
I had used
to turn my plain Jane wife
into a bombshell,
the same necromancy
that has ruined my life.

She's gorgeous
and uninhibited,
has become a paramour
to the underbelly,
living out bitter fantasies
long buried.
Every man wants her
and she needs them all

to fill the hole
I helped create.

I stepped out
of the shadows
pushing her lover away,
tossing the dust
over both of us.
I took her hand.
The enchanted glitter
settled on our skin
as I silently wished
for her life
to be better.
Under a pawn shop light
she transformed
into the girl
I had married
while
I disappeared.

prompt: The void

Absolute Zero

The void opened up
spilling restive gemstones of light
in front of me,
a checkerboard
of blue and red
telling me double stories
of which path to take.
I looked for the markers
you surely left behind
so I could follow,
but the stars put a finger
to their lips
and whispered in a hush
“Shh, we’ll never tell.”
Left, right, left, right,
I jumped from one blue giant
to another
searching for your perfume
or the distant echo
of your voice.
“Shh, we’ll never tell,”
the stars laughed behind my back
as I changed
to the reds,
yearning for your heat,
finding only the
absolute zero

of the void.
The lush, malevolent night
opened up to me
spilling singing gemstones,
their light a siren's call
leading me away
from the mercies of
forgetting the feel
of the small of your back
and the look in your eyes
when I said your name.

prompt: Feeling lost

Imaginary Lines

The horizon marks me
as one
who needs help,
my boat sailing
for no shore,
no landing in sight,
paint a canvas
in the pointillist style
and I am
in every dot,
crying for the Sun to set
on the water,
melted gold
weaving a path
for me to follow
until it disappears
in the rushing darkness.
Once more
I am adrift,
the line of demarcation
out of reach
like a true
earthly purpose.
I have been marked
as someone
the continents
have no use for

and the seas
bury like treasure.
Take a fast sloop,
a rusted dhow,
fly a seaplane
from island to island,
please come for me
before the horizon
cuts me in two.

prompt: secrets and dreams

Hi Fi

A song plays in my head
on a cheap, old
record player,
each pop and hiss
a ghost on my skin.
The opening of *Rats in the Cellar*
makes me twelve again
reading the liner notes
on the album jacket
while trying to understand
the lyrics,
each word
as big a mystery to me as
the girl in third period
I can't stop staring at.
My driving route
becomes grooves on a record,
I'm looping in circles
ever tighter,
skipping over warps
in the record,
moving closer to home.
The last song of the album
plays in my head
crackling from the tinny speakers
like a bonfire
warming my face

more than the girl
that sparkled in my eyes.
The song ends,
the needle lifts,
side one is over.
I sit in silence,
settle my eyes on row 4, seat 1
waiting for class to start.

prompt: emergence

In the Luminescence

Dystopian feelings,
wandering the graveyard
fetching loose change
for a cigarette,
If we look at the Sun
will we see ourselves
in our blindness
or stare longer
to increase the high?
I am in love
with the idea
of being meaningful,
but lead in my legs
keeps me grounded,
moving toward nothing,
drifting away,
a mylar balloon with
"I was here"
written on the side.
We stare at the moon
like feral dogs
searching for a master,
hoping the answer
not found in the day
will present itself
in the luminescence.

Muse 4

Inspired by stories in the news

The Names

The news presses on,
dreary upon dread,
a feast of the senseless.
Turn the pages,
tactile or electronic,
read the names with sorrow,
absorb them for
the following moments,

(Ed, Susan, Desean)

keep them warm
through prayers and tears,
we will never forget,
our pronouncement to the ether

(Terrell, Phyllis, Danny)

but tomorrow
there are new names
to read about,
new lives to mourn,
we will never forget

(Greg, Lorraine, Margaret)

until Wednesday
when the next batch

capture our attention,
drain our empathy,

(Maddie, Darrell, Lisa)

leave us lost,
backs buckling under the weight
of all the names.

Set List

They encountered the gunman
    in the hallway
    as they walked to their room,
    laughing at Cindy's joke,
    discussing what songs
    they hoped to hear
    at the concert later that night.
    He nodded at the pretty girls
    as he walked past,
    they didn't notice him.
They encountered the gunman
    outside while Dave
    had a smoke
    and snorted his way
    through a story
    about the flight in
    and the woman who
    got stuck in the bathroom.
    They didn't realize
the man in the gray baseball cap
was listening and laughing along.
They encountered the gunman
    in the parking lot
    using a broken metal coat hanger
    to get into a Dodge van.
    The young policemen
    checked his license and registration
    and they could see the keys
    dangling from the ignition.

The officers used
their own slim jim
to assist,
leaving without finding
the guns and ammunition
hidden in the back.
They encountered the gunman
at 9:16 p.m.
during the band's second song
when the bullets
made in his basement
ripped through their flesh.
They fell to the ground,
the strum of the guitar
still in their ears,
the beat of the drums
still rumbling through their chest.
They encountered the gunman
on a night filled with excitement,
anticipation, music
and community,
when the stars in the sky
made promises
to lifelong friends
and newly met lovers
that were sealed
by 10,000 voices
singing in unison
to a song that felt
written just for them.
They encountered the gunman
under a three quarters full moon
on the worst night of his life

when all the collected anger
exploded from his heart
into a statement
no one will hear
over the sound of the screams.

3,000 Seagulls

landfall

from chaos amid a listing ship
they fly to land
sun-kissed and dappled with blooms,
blooms of color and
real flesh,
a morning's worth of salvation
in an evening of late-heard prayers

in the water

the ship slips under
surface waves,
drowning the cries of the remaining
who stopped
counting their breaths
when the mast and sail
were lost beneath

the seagulls

from chaos they flew
to paradise,
escaping to the father
on halcyon winds
looking back
only to mourn

Endless Clips of Ammo

Serial killer in Toronto
Two police officers shot in Colorado
Homeless men gunned down in Las Vegas
Good morning,
time to go out into a world
that waits for you
with a mouthful of fangs
and endless clips of ammo.

Five headless bodies in Mexico
13 year old girl stabbed
Football player run down by drunk driver
Walk out your front door
into a world
that hates you.
Drink your morning coffee
to stay alert
for the one
that has your name.

Earthquake in Taiwan
Hurricane in Puerto Rico
Typhoon in Indonesia
Work all day with one eye
glancing over your shoulder,
speak to others
but don't say the wrong word.

Tax cuts for the rich, but not for you
Health insurance for senators, but not for you
A raise for congress, but none for you
Drive home,
comfortable in the knowledge
that no one
is going to help you.

Go to sleep with a prayer
or an upraised middle finger,
whichever helps you cope,
knowing that during the night
the world will keep spinning
toward oblivion.

Pusher

She's gone now,
taken to and from,
worlds apart,
left this one
for peace.
Our world,
the one that pushed her
didn't even take a moment,
no apologies,
no regrets.
Our world is a bully
streaked in the yellow
of cowardice
but believing that
or saying it out loud
doesn't help her
or us.
She's gone now,
pushed away
to the only peace
she could find.

Reading About the Rock Star's Relapse

Reading about the rock star's relapse
reminds me of her
and I wonder
how she is
while we all sit around
our tv's at night,
confident and proud
that we're ok.

I'll dream of her
again tonight probably,
and I hope it will be better
than the previous night
when I couldn't be forgiven
and woke up wondering
what was real.

Muse 5

Word randomly chosen from the dictionary

Insomnia: chronic inability to sleep

The Howling

The daylight sparkles
with chips of night,
the darkness
is spun
with sunbeams,
a world of wanderers
trip through
the stripes
spinning tales
to one another
of loss
and eidolons in blue.

Seeing the crossroads
through the kitchen window
the call is sent
to the Man himself,
ready to make a deal
for unconsciousness,
my flesh
for sleeping bones,
a star that isn't mine
for the moon
that isn't either.

I've run the risk
of being late

for everything,
of being lost
forever,
to make it about
something else
but awake or asleep,
divine or profane,
the howling inside
remains the same.

Gloom: Partial or total darkness or an atmosphere of melancholy or depression

A Hole in the Gloom

The rain slowed to a mist
that held on for its life
as day turned to evening.
I sat on the porch
staring through a hole
in the shifting gloom,
trying to see the other side,
an oasis in the drudgery.

A 90s style Corvette sped down the road,
driven by a man too old
to handle his late-life toy,
spraying rainwater
in all directions,
erasing my vision
of the promise.
When solitude returned,
low-hanging, fast-moving clouds
obscured my glimpse,
an upturned middle finger
to my dreams
of finding a way across.

I stuck out a feeble hand,
reaching for a hold,
any grasp of something better,

but the opening in the heaviness
had closed,
dark rain returned unwelcome
bringing with it cold
that pierced my arthritic fingers.
I went back inside
my hollow home,
the closing of the door
like a dull church bell
signaling the end.

falconry: the sport of hunting with falcons or other birds of prey; the keeping and training of such birds

Above the Pines

An outstretched arm,
a safe place to land,
from overtop I see neither.

The clouds guide me away
across the Carolina-blue sky
to a palace unknown.

My instinct is to return,
search the spotted ground
for my stake in this world.

A grind of intrusive thoughts
bring me level with a meadow
of goldenrod and Timothy grass.

Home is familiar with repetition,
and the promise of praise,
a soft night in soft company.

Gliding on a slipstream,
I capture a spirit
I didn't know existed.

No safe place to land,
no mannered voice in the tissue of my ear,
I soar above the pines.

overbear: 1. to crush or press down upon with physical force 2. to prevail over, as if by superior weight or force; dominate

Bonecracker

At night,
in bed,
under the weight
of the ceiling overhead,
I search the rolling darkness
for the truth,
and the silence
is a reckoning.

taxi dancer: a girl employed, as by a dance hall or night-club, to dance with the patrons for a fee

When it Was All Right

I pay for a dance.

In the darkness of the club
I feel the heat from her body.

My eyes stare over her head
at the colored lights
strung on the walls,
my left hand presses against her back,
wishing it was your form
under the dress.

I'm not a dancer,
so she is leading awkwardly,
my feet following
while the rest of my body
floats in circles.

When the music ends,
we part,
exchanging shy smiles.

***

You and I went dancing once
when the world

was still black and white.
I'm missing your kisses on my neck
and the press of your breasts.

I paid for a dance.

I needed more to forget.

Muse 6

observing the behavior of other people

Fairweather Street

Houses dot the landscape,
family dwellings
holding the American dream of
mom, dad and 2.5 children.
"Don't forget me," says Maxi
the golden retriever
and we all laugh.
Infrastructure delineates one side of the street
from the other,
roads, bridges and right-of-ways,
the lines separating chaos.
A new house has just been built
waiting for a new family,
an addition to the neighborhood,
a mystery.
Will they be friend or foe?
The birds and squirrels don't care,
but the couple across the street does.
It's quiet now
but after they move in
the kids might scream,
the TV may blare,
maybe the husband and wife will fight,
life on Fairweather Street hangs in the balance.
Houses fill the landscape,
family dwellings
lost inside the American dream.

That Edge

"I know, I'm going to hell,"
my friend always says
after telling one of his jokes
that make me laugh
and cringe
at the same time.
He gets away
with saying things
I never could.
I wonder sometimes
if I secretly
want to be him,
just for a moment,
to exist inside
that edge,
feel the blade
slice my skin
and draw blood.
Someone pours alcohol
in the wound
to punish me
for my sin,
but I don't repent.
I laugh harder
than everyone else
feeling my horns
form under the skin.

Serfs of Walmart

The drudgery of the day
brought me here,
a parking lot
in the rain,
where good people
and bad
congregate to commune,
vend, consume and rest
before returning to lives
brought under
by commonality and normalcy.
Here, for a moment,
we can feel better about ourselves
because of the car we drive
compared to the guy who
pulled in next to us.
We can judge the clothes
or shoes of others
to build our pedestal.
Their cheap hair cut
primps the cushion
of our throne
and how they speak or behave
creates a twisted ladder
for us to climb to the top
of our tower to sit
in judgment.
For a few minutes
we are the king or queen

of our realm.
But when we start our car engine
and pull out
back to our life
we are us again;
errands, problems,
tension, worries;
our tower crumbles,
throne cleaved in two.
We are them and
they are us,
the kingdom laid bare.

Reunion

Some were smiling
in the picture,
a few looked tired,

five former friends
at a party,
none knowing the others
would be there,

a forced congregation
at the
'everybody smile' altar.

Behind them,
balloons
reached for the ceiling,

searching for escape
from the room
with no oxygen.

Summer Concert Season (Reflections before Aerosmith)

They come for the music
and spectacle.
Some come to be seen,
muscles bulging out of tank tops,
breasts pressed tight
against a blouse two sizes too small.

They come for the music
and to hide in the parking lot,
hide with bottles and baggies
and pipes and friends who
won't make it.

They come for the music,
can't wait for it to start,
scream for it to start,
when will they come on stage?
I can't scream much longer.
There they are! Yeah!
Scream . . . scream . . . scream
drowning out the music
you came to hear.

They come for the music
and overpriced shirts
to prove to the tribe they were there
and overpriced beers because
its beer and its available

so it must be consumed
and overpriced food
because there is still money in their pocket.

They come for the music.
Oh, was there music?

Muse 7

The night sky

Saturn's Rings

the stars flash blue
in the spotlight
of my attention

the show begins now
the moon as MC
one constellation clapping

I want to see a shooting star
but their tour
is over Europe for the summer

the house lights are down
I take my seat
with the VIPs

Aldebaran opens with a joke
does an impression of Pegasi 51
closes with a song

Saturn's rings
Jupiter's red spot
the show goes on

Alien Invasion

Dirt road,
3:34 a.m.,
alone in the truck,
staring at the sky.
It stares back,
winking eyes of
blue-tinged and
red-hued light
making me feel
like I should apologize
for eavesdropping.

I wanted
to ask a question,
but the heavens
keep their secrets
from all but a
chosen few.

I Have Seen the Moon

I have seen the moon
in baby blue skies
playing a hide and seek game
as shadow and light,
winking when caught
peering over my shoulder.

I have seen the moon
as a cusp,
splitting the fabric
with an orange eye
allowing me a glimpse
of the past.

I have seen the moon
in a cock-eyed grin,
playing the fool
for all,
to remind us
of his impending visit.

I have seen the moon
in half-faced mourning
for the light it leaves behind,
stubborn darkness remains
like black sand
in the ancient craters.

I have seen the moon
in bulging splendor,
pregnant with ice-blue silk,
shaking off bursts
of carved dust
into a hazy gray-black sky.

I have seen the moon
hung like an ornament
off of a coal-black branch,
the character-making pock marks
painted on
by an astral brush.

I have seen the moon
in harvest hay,
in golden summer slumber,
in winter's frozen void.

I have seen the moon
wide-eyed and in dreams.
The old man
charms and haunts me
until he is all I see.

The Ancient Void

On an eternal flight
through space-time
their voices
follow me
through wormholes,
past supernovas
and the heat
from a nascent star.
I live
with the voices
as a tail
latched onto my spirit.

I will exist forever
among the worlds,
between the galaxies,
in the dark matter,
a child of
the ancient void
but I will never forget,
never release,
never ignore
the voices
of my home's past,
the people of Earth,
billions who lived
and perished,
remain with me.

I am a comet
of energy
and remembrance,
on a journey
to introduce the universe
to us,
tell it our names,
replay our voices
as we speak of
life, death,
music and language,
adventures and dreams.
The strings that
formed us
and the particles
that bound us
will be known throughout
the ancient void.

Pluto's Necklace

Spinning through the void
of space and time,
swallowed by Einstein's
curved thoughts,
my mind stretches before me
like a rope unraveling to form
pearl-like strings of brain cells
that helix and dive
into tunnels of extrapolated theory
and packets of
mathematical conjecture.
The chains of gray matter
drag me along
like a pendant,
an ornament for the universe.

A Song for Sedna

The man on the mountain
sings for
the clouds
that are his shelter.

The clouds in the sky
sing for
the Earth
that holds them close.

The Earth revolves
singing for
mother Sun
as she heats its rocky surface.

Mother sun
sings for
herself,
praises for the life giver
and withholder.
Her song is heard
all the way to Sedna.

The frigid rock in space,
abandoned and without
light or heat,
sings for
revenge.

Muse 8

observing social media

This Concludes Our Broadcast Day

This is an exclusive presentation of my
you-have-to-be-shitting-me face,
made possible by
your idiotic comments,
also sponsored by
my invisible apathy
toward manure
presented as
a tasty treat.
Join me again tomorrow,
same time, same channel
for a new episode
because I think
in the next 24 hours
your show called
"Moron Shares Dumb Opinions
with no Basis in Facts"
will still be on the air
and I'll need to respond.

The Great White

Give me a line
to say,
I'll act out
my rage
for the paying audience.
Stage left or stage right,
give me a direction
and I'll huff and puff
like a bull,
trampling your ideas
that aren't as good as mine.
Put my name
at the top of the marquee,
big letters,
bold and in red,
so it bellows
me
and only me.
Rent me a billboard
so I tower over everyone
like an alabaster god.
I am the disenfranchised
white male,
hear me bloviate,
make me a sandwich
and elect me to
a government office.

Making a Point in 2025

Full of holes
and downstream,
the preamble to my rant
is drowning
among the trout.
I will be heard though,
whether my voice be a whisper
or amplified through
a Marshall stack.
The speech is written
in Klingon
so no one can understand it,
even me,
but it is brilliant,
a quasar of energy
among a field of brown dwarf stars,
a clean patch of grass
in a field of shit.
I will be heard
even if I make no sense.
Going live on social media in
3 . . . 2 . . . 1

The World Engine

Double down
and make it all
about you,
that's how
the world engine
runs today.
Your thoughts
are not as important
as mine,
your clothes, please,
I might wear that
on a Facebook pic
If I still used
that archaic platform.
If you're over 40,
no wait, now it's 30,
then why are you
trying to be relevant?
Who's Paul McCartney
and what is a Beatle?
The Rolling who? They're 80!
This is our time
and always will be
because we aren't
going to get old.
We'll always be cool
or whatever word
we're using this week.

The Age of Dissemination

Every opinion
must be spoken
out loud
into a microphone
and in front of
a camera,
recorded for all to hear
and bask in
its profundity.

We must all be subjected to
everyone else's each move
and thought
and then comment
on them
so others
may comment on
our comments
and assess
our comments
so they may
comment on them.

No one will be spared
the banality of anything
or anyone,
keep no desire
to yourself,
don't rob the world

of a single breath
or bowel movement.
If we are to survive
we must know all,
see all
and respond to all.

This is the
Age of Dissemination,
open your hearts and minds
to receive the gifts,
prepare for your fame
and the backlash
it will bring,
respond to the attacks,
show no humility
or understanding,
belligerence and vitriol
rule the day
followed closely
by ego and stupidity.

This is another
Golden Age
and we are all
the stars
we were never
meant to be
with an audience
that can't
tell the difference.

Muse 9

Music
(all of the songs that inspired me are available to listen to on YouTube)

written while listening to *Varuna* by Vas

The Church of All Who Remain

They moved somehow
in tandem,
    the faces in the blood,
baleful eyes
furrowing a moat
into my skin,
filling the channel
with ancient dhows
to keep me still.
The audience clapped politely,
wavering support
    for the play in progress,

but in the desert
Bactrian symphonies
    started the march
of the clans
out of Eden,
into the copious sea of stars,
the magnitude of the multitude
leading the followers
away in chains.

The faces floated down
    onto the surface
of the water
as the oasis was abandoned

for a lesser narrative
with a restive denouement.
The lateen rigs are on the horizon,
my moat emptied of hired guns,
allowing me to lead or follow.

My spirit is indecisive
while the sand
rises past my knees
like floodwater.
I make my final soliloquy,
    impassioned and forlorn,
to the gathering of saints
and the church of all who remain behind.

written while listening to *Hymns of the Winterlight* by Foglord

Away

Dreamaway,
voices talking over one another,
the reception is bad,
bend the rabbit ears
to get channel 27
so we can watch
The Thing from Another World again.

Fallaway,
I can't remember much,
only scraps
that don't make much sense,
too much of my childhood
has escaped into the ether
never to return,
even the good stuff
with Mom holding my hand.

Thataway,
riding on a brown and white horse
through the desert
searching for the only water
in a hundred miles,
I'm dying of thirst.
yet won't stop for you
nor the boogie man.

Faraway,
each day becomes its own nest
of straw and sticks
that won't stay together
in the wind and rain,
falling apart,
tumbling to the hard ground
with no grace
and less measure.

Away,
there I am,
in the back of the room,
seen and unseen
at the same time,
righteous and profane
to only a few,
misshapen to others,
a mystery to myself.

written while listening to *Beethoven's Fifth symphony*

Palms Up

From dark to light
and back again,
shades and shadows
play their games
until the applause
scares them into the corners.
We can win our freedom,
and move with grace
through this world
if we recognize
the darkness has its place
and time,
but when we
straighten our backs
the light must come forward
to glow
in the palms of our hands.

written while listening to *Desert Winds of Change* by Steve Roach

Brown Noise

I lie on my back at night,
staring at the ceiling.
and imagining
where I'll be tomorrow
when I live
Thursday number 3024.
Will I be in the past
or the future
while my present
languishes under my fingers?

The brown noise
from my ambient sound app
plays with the folds.
of my brain,
massaging me to sleep,
a whisper before I'm under
makes me wonder
why the darkness
never lets go.

2:34 a.m.
and I wake up,
momentarily misremembering
what Mom had said
before she passed.

A spiteful voice from the dark
reminds me
I didn't get to her bedside in time.
If she said anything,
the ether captured it,
holding the precious words hostage
from my past-obsessed mind.

4:10 a.m.
My eyes open,
the phantoms
of the vengeful night
steeling the last foam
of a dream.
I get up to use the bathroom,
and the dream is already gone.
Someone had been with me,
we were walking
but nothing else remains.

In the mirror
my eyes look puffy.
I have two hours
before I get up for work,
my life hours
evaporating like morning fog.
The dream feels important,
but it won't return.

The brown noise
pulls the taffy of
my consciousness apart,
handing the irregular strips

to the god of sleep.
I don't see where he hides them
before I am gone
to the world
of the afterthought,
waiting for 6 a.m.
and another Thursday.

written while listening to the self-titled album by *Box of Frogs*

Unseen

I am followed
by a version of myself
that exists in the foggy shadows,
but never in flesh.
He hounds me,
disrupts my sleep,
changes my taste in music
to something I used to hate.
I can feel his disapproving eyes
dragging me to paths
I refuse to take
and his frustration is palpable.
I am not him
and he is not me,
he does not wish we were one,
his only desire
is to switch my light
for his shadows,
to be alive,
in a way I'm not.
My watcher has no fears,
while I live
in the belly of the beast,
his desires
dwarf mine,
his heat
roils the fabric of space.

No step I take lands
without him filling in
the footprint
with hoary fog,
his vacant lungs trying to breathe
so a feather for a tongue
can tickle my mind
with ideas
meant for someone else.
I am always followed
by a version of myself
that cries out for more
of a life I cannot give him.

written while listening to *The Ubiquitous Mr. Lovegrove* by Dead Can Dance

Dream-Song

Red
    January moon
        silent in repose

The singer's
    honey baritone
            awakens

A snake charmer's
    hypnotic aria
        entwines

The rhythms
    enter my veins
        replacing the blood

My wings flutter
    soughing a message
        to the firmament

I am a prisoner
    of sober words sung
        in tempting isolation

My cries to heaven
are drowned out
by an unseen timbrel

The dream-song is unending
the snake's fangs
have bitten deep into my flesh

Are there more people
and languages
still unspoken?

The answers are hidden
not on my tongue
I have been muted

February
will be blue
with no moon

Muse 10

Writing a poem in a different form from what you normally do. I mainly write freestyle so the poems that follow are in structured forms

haiku: a Japanese poem of seventeen syllables, in three lines of five, seven, and five.

sunspots here and there
puddles of light dot the porch
I hide in the shade

names etched into glass
the arch of green and gold glows
souls of the past sing

a call on the phone
the voice whispers hello friend
memories flood back

cicadas singing
twilight takes over again
everything slows down

tanka: a Japanese poem of thirty-one-syllables, best known in its five-line, 5/7/5/7/7 syllable count form.

sad eyed tiger stares
outside his bare habitat
freedom is a dream
late night mistake by handler
and he is gone fur aflame

I have the desire
to go on an adventure
to see something new
I also like staying home
introvert problems again

Acknowledgments

"Drinking in the Dusk" was originally published in the *In Gilded Frame* anthology in 2013

"The Boatman" was originally published in *Song of Eretz* in 2014

"Overnight" was originally published in *Otherwise Engaged* in 2025

"A Brief Interruption" was originally published in *Down in the Dirt* in 2012

"Broad Shoulders" was originally published in *CC&D Magazine* in 2022

"Shifting" was originally published in the *Of Sun and Sand* anthology in 2013

"Alchemy" was originally published in the *Make a Wish* anthology in 2013

"Imaginary Lines" was originally published in *Hour of Writes* in 2017

"Hi Fi" was originally published in *Pyrokinetic* in 2016

"Fairweather Street" was originally published in *Chicago Record* in 2021

"That Edge" was originally published in *Song of Eretz* in 2014

"Serfs of Walmart" was originally published in *Eye on Life* in 2015

"Reunion" was originally published in *Dead Snakes* in 2015

"Summer Concert Season" was originally published in *The Swamp* in 2003

"Saturn's Rings" was originally published in *Syzygy Magazine* in 2015

"Alien Invasion" was originally published in the *Adrift on the Cosmic Sea* chapbook in 2014

"I Have Seen the Moon" was originally published in the *Adrift on the Cosmic Sea* chapbook in 2014

"The Ancient Void" was originally published in *Illumen* in 2015

"Pluto's Necklace" was originally published in *Black Petals* in 2019

"This Concludes Our Broadcast Day" was originally published in *CC&D Magazine* in 2024

"The Great White" was originally published in *CC&D Magazine* in 2024

"Making a Point in 2025" was originally published in *CC&D Magazine* in 2017 as "Making a Point in 2017"

"The World Engine" was originally published in *CC&D Magazine* in 2024

"The Age of Dissemination" was originally published in *Nazar Look* in 2012

"Dream-Song" was originally published in *Illumen* in 2012

The first and third haikus and both tankas were originally published in *5-7-5 Haiku Journal* in 2025

"Hi Fi" was originally published in the *Secrets and Dreams* anthology in 2016

"In the Luminescence" was originally published in the *Emergence* anthology in 2016

"The Names" was originally published in *Otherwise Engaged* in 2024

"Set List" was originally published in *CC&D Magazine* in 2020

"Endless Clips of Ammo" was originally published in *Record Magazine* in 2020

"Reading About the Rock Star's Relapse" was originally published in the *Edged in Blue* chapbook in 2004

www.ingramcontent.com/pod-product-compliance
Ingram Content Group UK Ltd.
Pitfield, Milton Keynes, MK11 3LW, UK
UKHW041315190726
13845UKWH00025B/274

9 789363 544987